KU-521-430

In-line Skating

Kathy Galashan

Published in association with The Basic Skills Agency

Hodder & Stoughton

A MEMBER OF THE HODDER HEADLINE GROUP

Acknowledgements

Cover: Tipp Howell/Telegraph Colour Library

Photos: pp 3, 14, 24 Corbis; p 6 Telegraph Colour Library; p 10 John Powell/Retna; p12 Kenny McLeish; p 18 Steven Behr/Stockfile

Thanks to Rob Cole and Tim and Simon Bradbury for their help.

Every effort has been made to trace copyright holders of material reproduced in this book. Any rights not acknowledged will be acknowledged in subsequent printings if notice is given to the publisher.

Orders; please contact Bookpoint Ltd, 39 Milton Park, Abingdon, Oxon OX14 4TD. Telephone: (44) 01235 400414, Fax: (44) 01235 400454. Lines are open from 9.00–6.00, Monday to Saturday, with a 24 hour message answering service.
Email address: orders@bookpoint.co.uk

British Library Cataloguing in Publication Data
A catalogue record for this title is available from the British Library

ISBN 0 340 77520 3

First published 2000
Impression number   10 9 8 7 6 5 4 3 2 1
Year   2005 2004 2003 2002 2001 2000

Typeset by GreenGate Publishing Services, Tonbridge, Kent.
Printed in Great Britain for Hodder and Stoughton Educational, a division of Hodder Headline Plc, 338 Euston Road, London NW1 3BH, by Redwood Books, Trowbridge, Wilts

Contents

Check out the Glossary on page 27.
It explains words used in the book that
you may not have come across before.

In-line skating and rollerblading.
are the same thing.
Put on a pair of boots
and away you go.
There's a whole new world out there.

Skating is fast.
It's fun.
It's exciting.
You can do it on your own
or with your friends.
It's a great way to meet new people.

Learn the basics.
Once you feel good on wheels
there are different ways to go.
There is roller hockey.
There is speed skating.
You can go on in-line skating holidays.
You can enter competitions.

1 Getting Started

The first time you wear boots
it feels strange.
It helps if you can rollerskate or ice-skate.

Try to find a good skater
to go with you the first few times.
Or have one or two lessons.
It's easy to get bad habits
and hard to get rid of them.

You will need a pair of skates.
A new pair starts at around £80.
Go to a shop and look at what there is.
Some boots are hard, like ski boots.
Some boots are soft.
They are like trainers on wheels.
They don't last as well
but they are lighter, cooler
and more comfortable.

Skating is fun and you can meet lots of people.

The wheels are important.
If you are a beginner,
choose smaller 70 mm wheels.
These are easier to learn on.

You can buy a second-hand pair of skates
for about £25 to £50.
Look in small ads in papers.
Ask around and see what you find.
Then when you are hooked
you can buy the pair that suits you.

It's impossible to learn without falling.
You need protection.
The streets are hard.
Wear knee pads, elbow pads
and wrist guards.

2 Recreational Skating

You can skate along the road
or along paths in parks.
It's a great way to keep fit.
It exercises lots of muscles
but doesn't strain them.
Lots of sports people use in-line skating
as part of their work out.

It's fast too.
If you want to get somewhere,
skating is quicker than the bus.
It's often faster than a bike.
Also it's much more fun.

In-line skating is a fast and fun way to travel.

In-line skating is about fast, smooth skating.
It's about control.
Once you can move you need to stop.
The better you can stop,
the more control you have.
Once you can stop,
you can relax,
let yourself go.

In-line skating is about reading the road
and staying cool.
Anyone can go fast.
Can you go fast
and jump the cracks and drains?
Can you avoid the kid on the pavement?
Can you hit a downhill slope
and stop when you want?

3 Aggressive Skating

Do you want a challenge?
You need a lot of nerve.

Aggressive skating is about tricks.
It is using your skates
in all sorts of different ways.
You can jump, twist and turn
on ramps and on concrete.

You can grind on kerbs and ledges.
When you grind you don't use wheels.
You slide along.

To grind you need special skates.
They have a grind plate
between the second and third wheels.

You jump on a rail
and land on the grind plate.
You get into different positions
for different tricks.
Then you can switch
from one trick to another
on the same go.

When you start,
it is hard to land on the grind plate.
After a while it becomes second nature.
Then you are ready for different tricks.

You can grind on kerbs and ledges.

4 Skate Parks

You can go to skate parks.
They have ramps and street courses
where you can learn tricks.
They are a good place to meet people
and get tips.

There are different tricks for different ramps.
On 'vert' ramps you build up speed,
think of a trick and jump.
'Getting air' is jumping up high.
The higher you get,
the more time there is to twist and turn.

a

b

Moving into position on the vert ramp.

c

d

Using the ramp edge to twist your body round.

e

f

Completing the 'kind grind' trick.

On mini ramps the tricks
are about fancy footwork and grinds.

There are no rules.
When you are good
you pull tricks
your own way.
You put tricks together
and create your own style.

Style is looking good on skates.
It's making tricks look easy.
It's looking cool and relaxed.
It's landing on your boots
not on your bottom.

Style is about landing on your boots, not on your bottom!

5 The Streets

The streets are great for tricks.
There are special places
where skaters hang out.
But there are plenty of places
for you to find.
You can practise on steps and kerbs.
It helps to wax the surface.
Then you can slide along better.

6 Roller Hockey

Do you like team games?
Try roller hockey.
It's a hard game.
You need guts and nerve and skill.
You can play in a hall
or on an open space.
It's a very exciting game.

Roller hockey is played on skates
using sticks and a ball
or a rubber disc, called a 'puck'.

The aim of the game is to score goals.
The aim of the defence is to stop you.
You need at least four players
and a goalie for a team.

Physical tactics make the game what it is.
You can block, slam into
or trip up the scorer.
It's scary having four people on wheels
come straight at you.
To win, your team needs
to be faster and bolder
than the other team.

Roller hockey is a tough game.

The game is rough and tough.
Clothes are your only protection.
Apart from skates, you will need
shin pads and knee pads
to protect your legs.
Padded shorts and a box to
protect your privates
and lower back.
Body armour protects your chest and back.
Elbow pads are useful.
A neck brace and helmet protects your head.
The clothes are armour for the battle ahead.
You are not on your own.
You are part of a team.

7 What People Say About In-line Skating

Jo   My skates are part of me.
          I do a paper round in the mornings.
          It's fast and fun on skates.
          I skate to school,
          I skate to friends' houses.
          It's the quickest way to get anywhere.
          There's nothing like
          the whiz of skating empty streets
          early in the morning.

Sam   I used to rollerskate
so when I started
I found it quite easy.
The stopping was a problem.
I stopped by skating off the path onto grass
Sometimes I stopped
by crashing into a wall or falling over.
Then a friend showed me
how to use the brake pads.
Now I can stop frontwards, backwards,
at high speed or low speed.
PROGRESS!

Tim   I bought myself a scaffolding pole.
I set it up on two bricks
in front of the house.
It made a great rail.
I spent hours and hours
jumping on and trying to balance.
Then I set the rail up on milk crates.
I practised and practised.

I used to buy wax for the rails
to help me slide.
But wax is expensive –
so now I use soap.
It's just as good.

I started trying tricks.
I got myself a longer rail
so I could put tricks together.
First near the ground,
then higher.
It gave me the confidence
to go out on the streets
and try rails.

Simon   I love roller discos.
My friends and I skate around
having a good time.
There's loud music and flashing lights.
Going fast and good music
go great together.

Jane   I go in for competitions.
Competitions are advertised in magazines.
If I win, I can pick up a sponsor
and that makes me feel good.
There are different sections in competitions.
I usually enter the street course
because I'm best at rails and steps.

Skating fast and good music go well together.

Finding Out More

Magazines
Skatermag
Unity
DNA
These have pictures of tricks.
There are interviews with skaters.
There is news of competitions.
There is often a 'how to' section
with step by step photos of different tricks.
There is also a 'For Sale' section in the back.

Videos
Battle My Crew is a good one to start with
but there are lots to choose from.

In-line Skating Shops

Unity magazine has a list
of skate shops in the UK.
These sell everything you need.
Also the people who work there
know what is going on
and pass on local news and information.

The Internet

There is plenty to find and check out.
Search 'In-line Skating' and see what comes up.
The personal pages are fun, too.

Yahoo have a home page on 'In-line Skating'.
This connects to clubs, events, equipment
and personal pages.
Try: http://www.skatefaq.com/
        www.inliners.co.uk

Glossary of Terms Used

Aggressive skating Pulling tricks on skates. This can be on the street or in a skate park.

Grind plate A plastic plate between the second and third wheels under the boot.

Grinding Using the grindplate and chassis instead of the wheels.

Grinding trick This is when you do a trick and don't use the wheels.

Mini ramp A low ramp with curved sides.

Puck A rubber disc sometimes used in roller hockey (instead of a ball).

Ramp A slanting surface to skateboard on.

Recreational skating Skating along the roads or pavements.

Sponsor A company or person that gives you money in return for you advertising their goods or services.

Vert ramp A ramp with straight (vertical) sides. It is usually quite high.

Wax a surface To use wax or soap to make rails slippery.